EASY HALLOWEEN COLORING BOOK FOR KIDS

AGE 4-8

THIS BOOK BELONGS TO

HALLOWEEN

HAPPY Halloween

HALLOWEEN

BOO!

NAME: ....

HALLOWEEN

NAME: ....

HALLOWEEN

NAME: ....
SPOOKY

NAME: ....
SPOOKY

HORROR

HORROR

HALLOWEEN

R.I.P.

CHOCO
TRICK
OR
TREAT